KINGFISHER
LONDON & NEW YORK

Copyright © 2010 by Kingfisher
Published in the United States by Kingfisher,
175 Fifth Ave., New York, NY 10010
Kingfisher is an imprint of Macmillan Children's Books, London.
All rights reserved.

Illustrated by Kath Grimshaw
Concept by Jo Connor

Distributed in the U.S. by Macmillan, 175 Fifth Ave., New York, NY 10010
Distributed in Canada by H.B. Fenn and Company Ltd., 34 Nixon Road,
Bolton, Ontario L7E 1W2

LIBRARY OF CONGRESS CATALOGING-IN-PUBLICATION DATA
The book of—why? / [illustrated by Kath Grimshaw].
      p. cm.
  1. Science—Miscellanea—Juvenile literature. I. Grimshaw, Kath, ill.
II. Kingfisher (Firm)
    Q173.B6755 2010
    500—dc22

2010004747

ISBN: 978-0-7534-6396-3

Kingfisher books are available for special promotions and premiums.
For details contact: Special Markets Department, Macmillan,
175 Fifth Avenue, New York, NY 10010.

For more information, please visit www.kingfisherbooks.com

First published in 2010
Printed in China
10 9 8 7 6 5 4 3 2
2TR/0410/LFA/UNT/140GSM/C

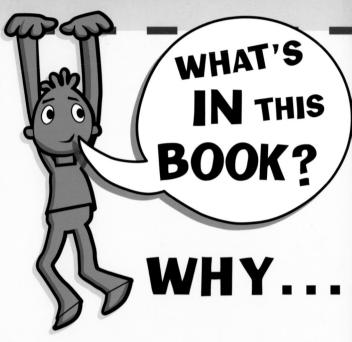

WHAT'S IN THIS BOOK?

WHY...

HAVE YOU EVER ASKED YOURSELF WHY?

It's only natural to be confused by the world around us . . . It is a very complicated and surprising place sometimes! And you'll never understand what's going on around you unless you ask yourself "WHY?" every now and again.

This is "why" we have made this book.

We have traveled over the land, under the sea, up mountains, across deserts—and even into outer space—to collect as many tricky questions as we could find . . .

. . . and we also found the answers for you!

We now invite you to come with us on our journey around the world of "WHY," so that we can show you all the answers that we discovered.

Did you know . . .

Not all trees lose their leaves. Conifers have tough leaves that can withstand the winter cold.

While we were searching for all those answers, we found out some other pretty interesting things, too. We wrote them all down on these panels so that you can memorize the amazing facts and impress your friends!

We also thought it might be fun to see how much of this shiny new knowledge you can remember—so at the back of the book, on pages 56 and 57, you'll find some Quick-Quiz questions to test you. It's not as scary as it sounds—we promise it'll be fun. (And besides, we've given you all the answers on pages 58 and 59.)

Are you ready for this big adventure? Then let's go!

QUICK-QUIZ QUESTIONS

1. What "y" holds you to the ground?
2. Earth is the third planet from the Sun. True or False?
3. What are premolars?
4. How deep underwater can humans dive?
5. What does chlorophyll use in order to make food for trees?
6. Conifer trees lose their leaves in the winter. True or False?
7. What is metamorphosis?
8. Unscramble RED BIRD WIND to show what reptiles use to keep out enemies.
9. Where did donsena insects come from?
10. Airplanes are good for the environment. True or False?
11. What helps fight germs in your body?

12. Which is lighter—warm or cold air?
13. Snakes have very good eyesight. True or False?
14. What is the biggest bird on Earth?
15. Unscramble COW REPT to show what force helps trees grip.
16. What is a baby hippopotamus called?
17. When did the dinosaurs die out?
18. Who invented cement to be used in building roads?

19. Who was king of the gods in ancient Greek stories?

20. Where did the first lot-on balloon ride take place?
21. What is the tallest mountain on Earth?
22. What is pollination?
23. How thick is Earth's water in winter?
24. Which sea is the saltiest?
25. Unscramble ICE IN EARTH to show what some animals do in the winter.

5

Astronauts have to wear seat belts to stop them from floating away when they go to the bathroom. Space toilets do not flush. Instead, everything is sucked away.

Astronauts on board a spacecraft can't feel gravity or see it working. Out in space, Earth's gravity is not strong enough to hold them down, so they float around like balloons.

WHY DO ASTRONAUTS FLOAT IN SPACE?

WHY IS EARTH SO SPECIAL?

Earth is the only planet in the solar system with water and living things on it. This is because it is the third planet from the Sun, and it gets just the right amount of heat and light. If it were any closer, it would be too hot. Any farther away, and it would be too cold.

WHY DO STARS TWINKLE?

Stars twinkle only when we look at them from Earth. As starlight travels toward us, it is bent and wobbled by movement in the air surrounding Earth, making the stars look like they are twinkling.

Did you know . . .

Sometimes flamelike sheets of glowing gas shoot out from a star. These are called prominences.

WHY DO DIVERS NEED HEADLIGHTS?

Did you know . . .

Humans can survive underwater without breathing for about nine minutes and can dive down to about 650 feet (200 meters).

Sunlight only reaches down to 650 feet (200 meters) below the surface of the ocean. This "sunlit zone" is where all sea plants and most sea animals live. From 3,280 feet (1,000 meters) onward, it is completely dark.

WHY DO TREES HAVE LEAVES?

Trees need their leaves in order to stay alive. Leaves contain a sticky green stuff called chlorophyll. Chlorophyll uses water, sunlight, and carbon dioxide in the air to make a sugary food. The food is then carried to every part of the tree in a sweet, gooey juice called sap.

Did you know . . .

In a single year, a forest of 400 trees gives off enough oxygen to keep at least 20 people breathing.

WHY DO LEAVES FALL IN THE FALL?

Big, green leaves make food while the Sun shines and the days are long. When the days get shorter, there is less time for making food, and the tree must live off its food reserves. Rather than also needing to feed their leaves, some trees shed their leaves in the fall.

Did you know . . .

Not all trees lose their leaves. Conifers have tough leaves that can withstand the winter cold.

11

WHY DO I FEEL DIZZY WHEN I SPIN AROUND?

In your ear, you have three loop-shaped tubes with liquid in them. This swishes around when you spin. Special nerves sense this movement and tell your brain that you are spinning. If you stop suddenly, the liquid continues to swish briefly. Your brain gets the wrong message, and you feel dizzy!

Did you know . . .

The smallest bone in the body is in the ear. It is called the stapes and is about 0.08 inches (2 millimeters) long.

WHY ARE EARS A FUNNY SHAPE?

The shape of your ears helps them catch sounds from the air. The sounds go through your earhole and into the hidden part, known as the inner ear, inside your head.

Did you know . . .

Ears have a drum in them. Your eardrum is a thin flap of skin that vibrates when sounds hit it.

KEY

1. Eardrum
2. Tiny bones
3. Spiral tube
4. Nerves leading to brain

WHY DO CATERPILLARS CHANGE INTO BUTTERFLIES?

Every caterpillar has to go through four different stages of development before it becomes a full-grown adult butterfly. At each stage, it changes its size, shape, and color.

Did you know . . .

Many types of insects change shape as they grow. This way of developing is called metamorphosis.

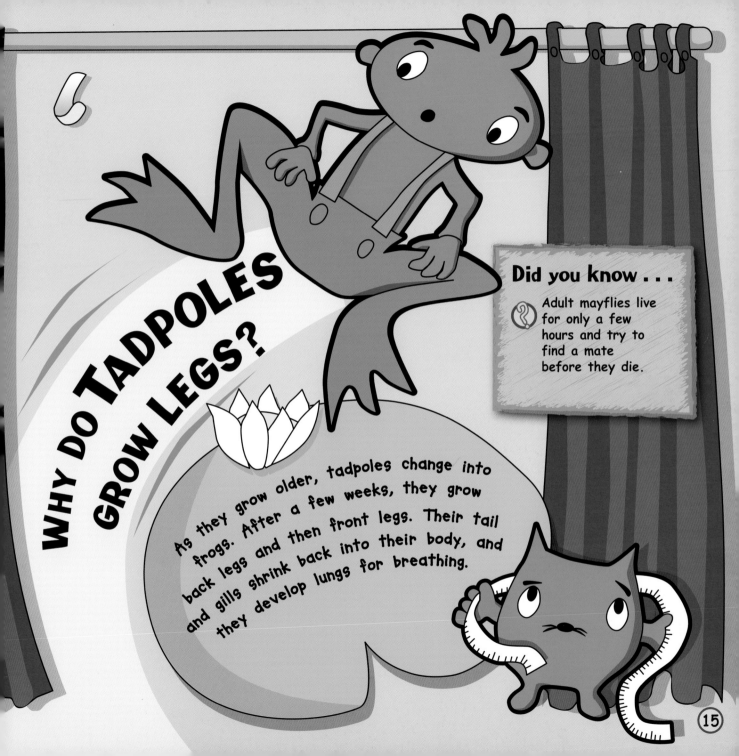

WHY DO TADPOLES GROW LEGS?

As they grow older, tadpoles change into frogs. After a few weeks, they grow back legs and then front legs. Their tail and gills shrink back into their body, and they develop lungs for breathing.

Did you know . . .

Adult mayflies live for only a few hours and try to find a mate before they die.

15

WHY DID CASTLES HAVE MOATS?

Did you know . . .

One way to beat enemies who shut themselves up in a castle was to surround it and wait for them to run out of food and water. This was called a siege.

Moats were deep, wide ditches filled with water that surrounded a castle. They made it difficult for enemies to break in to the castle. Friendly visitors could cross the moat over a drawbridge. But when enemies attacked, the drawbridge was raised so that they could not enter.

WHY DID KNIGHTS WEAR ARMOR?

During battle, knights were bashed and battered by weapons such as swords and axes. They had to protect their bodies from these sharp blades, so they wore suits of tough metal armor.

Did you know . . .

Japanese knights were called samurai. Their armor was made of metal plates attached to padded silk and leather.

WHY IS THERE A HOLE IN THE SKY?

High up in the atmosphere is the ozone layer, which absorbs most of the Sun's harmful rays. The ozone layer is damaged by chemicals called chlorofluorocarbons (CFCs for short), and a large hole has formed over Antarctica, letting in the damaging rays.

Did you know . . .

Jet planes fly in the ozone layer, between 6 and 25 miles (10 and 40 kilometers) above Earth's surface. Their engines release chemicals that damage the layer.

WHY IS SUNLIGHT WARM?

Did you know . . .

Things that allow heat to pass through them easily are called conductors. Some metals are excellent conductors.

Sunlight is warm because the Sun gives off heat as well as light energy. The Sun's heat energy travels toward us in straight, invisible lines called heat rays. You cannot see these rays, but you can feel them on your skin on hot, sunny days.

WHY DO I GET SICK?

Did you know . . .

Some germs like dirt. Washing your body and brushing your teeth help keep these germs away.

Tiny germs and bacteria enter our bodies and can make us sick. Our body is the perfect temperature for these germs to grow and multiply. To help you get better, your immune system produces antibodies to fight the germs. By eating healthily and staying active, you can reduce the risk of getting sick.

WHY DO MY TEETH CHATTER WHEN I'M COLD?

Did you know . . .

You do not have any nerves in your hair and fingernails. That is why it does not hurt when they are cut.

When you are cold, your muscles contract (become tighter) quickly to try and warm you up. This is called shivering. Your teeth chatter as the muscles in your jaw move.

WHY DO FLUTES HAVE HOLES?

To play the flute, you have to blow across the blowhole. The air makes its way down the tube, and you hear it come out as a musical sound. You change notes by covering and uncovering the different holes with your fingers.

Did you know . . .

A stringed instrument is tuned by turning the pegs at the end of its neck. Tightening a string makes a higher note and loosening it makes a lower note.

Did you know . . .

Air is invisible, so you cannot see the wind. But you can feel it on your face and see how it makes the trees sway.

WHY DOES THE WIND BLOW?

When you feel the wind blow, it's because air is moving. When the air is warm, it gets lighter and rises up into the sky. Cooler air then rushes in to take its place, creating a breeze.

23

WHY DOES A SNAKE FLICK OUT ITS TONGUE?

Did you know . . .

Even though they have bad eyesight, snakes can hunt in complete darkness. They can sense the body heat of a nearby animal and strike their prey with amazing accuracy.

As a snake's tongue darts in and out, it picks up scents in the air. The tongue carries these up to a sensitive area in the roof of the mouth, which "tastes" the air. These sensors then send messages to the brain, telling the snake whether a mate, a meal, or an enemy is near.

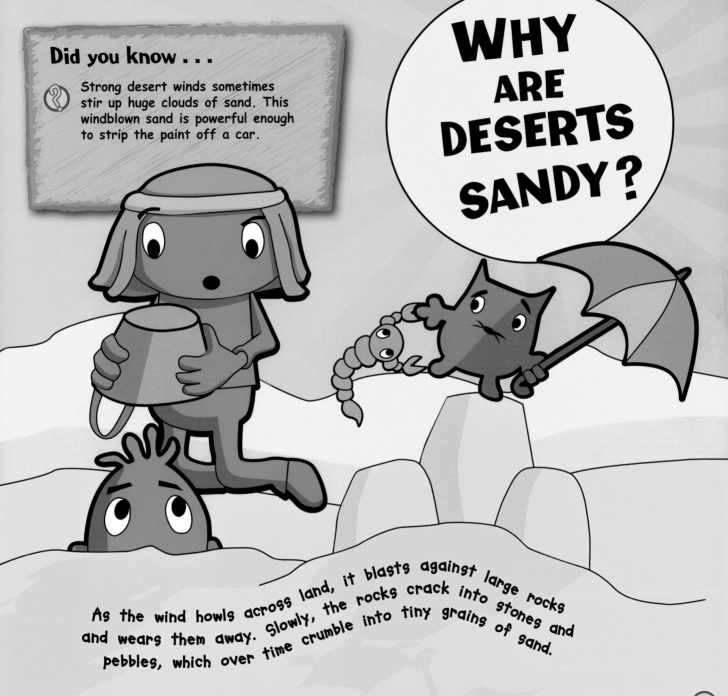

Did you know . . .

Strong desert winds sometimes stir up huge clouds of sand. This windblown sand is powerful enough to strip the paint off a car.

WHY ARE DESERTS SANDY?

As the wind howls across land, it blasts against large rocks and wears them away. Slowly, the rocks crack into stones and pebbles, which over time crumble into tiny grains of sand.

WHY DO GIRAFFES HAVE LONG NECKS?

A giraffe's long neck makes it tall enough
to eat the leaves at the top of trees.
Other animals cannot reach up as high, so
the giraffe has a lot to eat.

26

WHY CAN'T PENGUINS FLY?

Penguins cannot fly because their wings are too small to keep their heavy bodies up in the air. But penguins are very good swimmers and divers. They use their wings as paddles in the water.

Did you know . . .

The largest bird is the ostrich. It is too big to fly but can run at twice the speed of the fastest Olympic runners.

WHY DO BIKES HAVE TIRES?

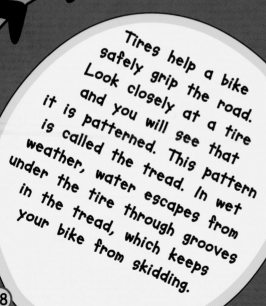

Tires help a bike safely grip the road. Look closely at a tire and you will see that it is patterned. This pattern is called the tread. In wet weather, water escapes from under the tire through grooves in the tread, which keeps your bike from skidding.

Did you know . . .

As a rubber tire rolls along, it rubs against the road. This rubbing creates a slowing force called friction, which helps the tire grip.

Horseshoes have been used as good luck charms for hundreds of years.

WHY DO HORSES WEAR SHOES?

Horseshoes help keep horses' hooves from being damaged by hard surfaces such as roads. The shoes are usually made of steel, and the person who makes and fits them is called a farrier.

29

Did you know . . .

The ostrich lays the heaviest eggs of any bird. Each egg can weigh up to 3 pounds (1.3 kilograms)—that's heavier than a bag of sugar.

WHY DO BIRDS LAY EGGS?

By laying babies inside eggs, a female bird can have several babies at once, and each one has a safe place in which to develop. When hatched, the babies can stay safely in the nest while their parents fly off to find food.

Did you know . . .

A female crocodile carries her babies in her mouth, being careful not to bite them with her razor-sharp teeth.

WHY DO KANGAROOS HAVE POUCHES?

A pouch is a safe place for a baby to grow. A newborn kangaroo is called a joey and is only the size of a peanut. After it is born, it struggles through its mother's fur until it reaches her warm pouch. There, it feeds on her milk and continues to grow.

WHY CAN I SEE THROUGH GLASS?

Did you know . . .

The Moon reflects light from the Sun. It has no light of its own.

You can see through glass because it is transparent. This means that it is almost clear, and it lets light shine through. Glass is great for windows because it lets sunlight into a room and also allows you to see what is happening outside.

WHY DO VOLCANOES BLOW THEIR TOPS?

Did you know . . .

Scientists who study volcanoes are called volcanologists or vulcanologists—after Vulcan, the Roman god of fire. This is also how volcanoes got their name.

Deep beneath an active, violent volcano is a giant chamber. Hot, runny rock and gases build up there until they blast upward, under immense pressure, through cracks in Earth's crust.

WHY ARE THERE NO DINOSAURS ON EARTH?

Did you know . . .

Many animals are "endangered," meaning that they are in danger of dying out, often because people have hunted too many of them.

The dinosaurs lived on Earth for millions of years. Then, about 65 million years ago, they became extinct—every single one of them disappeared. No one really knows why, but one idea is that a massive meteorite hit Earth and wiped them out.

WHY DO SPIDERS SPIN WEBS?

Did you know . . .

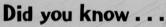

Most of the webs that you see are round "orb" webs, spun by garden spiders. Other spiders spin webs with different patterns.

Spiders spin webs to catch food. When an insect flies into the web, it gets stuck. The spider then rushes out to spin silk around it, and the insect turns into a liquid mush. Later, the spider can suck it up, like a drink!

Did you know . . .

Many people think that Tyrannosaurus could have run as fast as 30 miles (50 kilometers) per hour when chasing a meal.

WHY WAS TYRANNOSAURUS A BIGMOUTH?

Tyrannosaurus was a huge meat eater. At about 20 feet (6 meters) high, it stood three times taller than a grizzly bear today. Its mouth was so big that it could swallow a person whole!

37

Did you know . . .

The Romans invented concrete by mixing lime, water, and ash from volcanoes. Concrete is as strong as stone, and it sets hard, even underwater.

WHY WERE ROMAN ROADS SO STRAIGHT?

The Romans were excellent engineers. They used measuring instruments to figure out where the road should go and chose the shortest, straightest route between two camps, forts, or towns. These roads linked up the entire empire.

WHY WERE THE OLYMPICS HELD?

Did you know...

At the original Olympic Games, all athletes were naked. The Greeks were proud of their bodies and were not afraid to show them off.

The Olympic Games were part of a religious festival in honor of Zeus, the king of the gods. Every four years, thousands of people flocked to Olympia—a place in ancient Greece—to watch athletes and compete in games such as running, wrestling, and chariot racing.

39

WHY DO HOT-AIR BALLOONS FLOAT?

Did you know . . .

The first-ever balloon passengers were a rooster, a duck, and a sheep! Their eight-minute flight took place over Paris, France, in 1783.

The air inside a hot-air balloon is heated by a burner. When the air becomes warmer, it starts to rise because it is lighter than cold air. As the hot air rises, so does the balloon!

Did you know . . .

There are even taller mountains in space than there are on Earth. Olympus Mons on the planet Mars is three times higher than Mount Everest, the tallest mountain on Earth.

Only the highest mountains have snow on top. When water gets very cold, it freezes and turns into snow or ice—and the higher up you go on a mountain, the colder it gets.

Did you know . . .

Many trees and grasses spread their pollen in the wind. They don't need animal visitors, so they don't grow bright flowers.

WHY DO PLANTS HAVE FLOWERS?

Many plants have colorful, perfumed flowers that attract insects and other animals. When they feed on the sweet nectar inside the flower, they pick up a fine yellow dust called pollen, which they carry to another flower. When the pollen rubs off on the second flower, new seeds are made. This is called pollination.

42

WHY DO WE CUT DOWN TREES?

Did you know . . .

The tiger is one of many animals that are in danger of dying out because their forest homes are being destroyed.

Throughout history, people have cut down trees for their wood. Forests are also destroyed to clear land for farming and to build towns and cities.

WHY DO LEOPARDS HAVE SPOTS?

Did you know . . .

The fur of some animals that live in cold countries is brown in the summer and white in the winter. This makes it more difficult to see the animals in the winter, when snow covers the ground.

A leopard's spots help it hide among the trees and bushes so that it can jump out and surprise its prey. The light and dark markings in its fur match the patches of sunlight and shadow under the leafy branches.

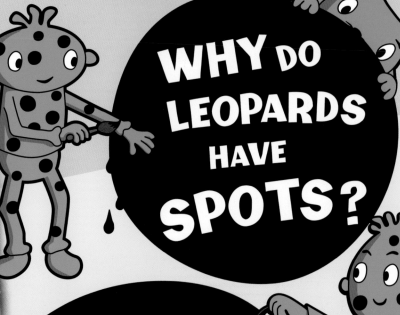

Did you know . . .

Mosquitoes are attracted to humans by their smell. They especially like the scent of hot, sweaty feet!

WHY DO SKUNKS STINK?

If a skunk feels threatened by a predator, it sprays a smelly, sticky fluid at its attacker's eyes. The liquid smells so bad that it can make the predator sick, allowing the skunk to escape.

WHY ARE OCTOPUSES LIKE JET PLANES?

Octopuses, squids, cuttlefish, and scallops all use jet propulsion to move. Octopuses pump water in over their gills and squirt it out through a fleshy tube called a siphon. They steer by pointing the siphon in different directions.

Did you know . . .

Some types of fish can "walk." Batfish have a pair of long, thick fins underneath their body. They use them to creep over the bottom of the ocean.

46

WHY DO WHALES SING?

Whales are talkative animals. They bellow, grunt, yelp, and make bubbling noises to find other whales and send messages. Male humpback whales sing long tunes, sometimes repeating them for hours or even days. This is probably to attract a mate.

Did you know . . .

Each bird has its own special song. Birds recognize each other by their songs, just as humans recognize friends by their voices.

WHY DO ANIMALS SLEEP IN THE WINTER?

Did you know . . .

Many animals grow thick coats of fur in the winter to help them survive the bitter cold.

For some animals, sleeping is the best way to survive the hungry winter days. Chipmunks, squirrels, hedgehogs, and some bears eat as much as they can in the fall and then hibernate (sleep) somewhere safe until the spring.

49

Did you know . . .

About 97 percent of Earth's water is salty. The remaining 3 percent is fresh water, which humans and animals drink.

WHY IS THE SEA SALTY?

Seawater tastes salty because it has salt in it! The same type of salt is used on food. Most of it comes from rocks on the land. Rain washes the salt into rivers, which carry it to the sea.

Did you know . . .

It is easier to float in salty seawater than it is in fresh water. The Dead Sea in the Middle East is the world's saltiest sea—swimmers cannot sink in it, even without water wings!

WHY DO WATER WINGS HELP ME FLOAT?

When you blow up your water wings, you are putting lots of air inside them. Air is much lighter than water, so it helps you float.

51

Did you know . . .

Early explorers figured out how fast they were traveling by timing how long it took a floating object in the water to pass by the full length of their ship.

WHY DID EXPLORERS OFTEN GET LOST?

Ancient maps were mainly the result of guesswork because people knew so little about the world. World maps did not begin to improve until the 1500s, when explorers began to make around-the-world voyages.

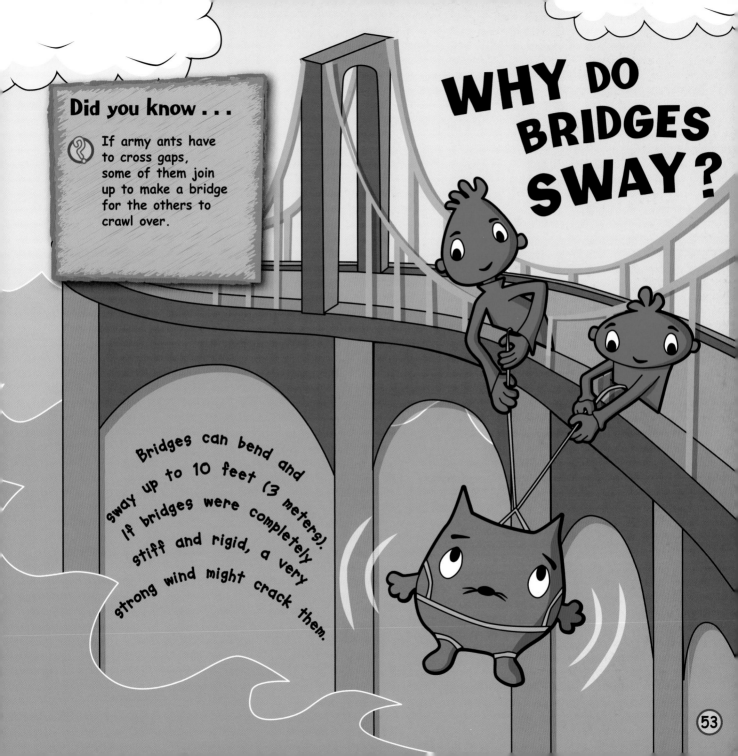

WHY DO BRIDGES SWAY?

Did you know . . .

If army ants have to cross gaps, some of them join up to make a bridge for the others to crawl over.

Bridges can bend and sway up to 10 feet (3 meters)! If bridges were completely stiff and rigid, a very strong wind might crack them.

WHY DO SHIPS FLOAT?

Did you know . . .

Humans blink every two to ten seconds, and each blink takes about 0.3 seconds. This means that you spend about 30 minutes every day with your eyes shut.

WHY DO GLASSES HELP YOU FOCUS?

Did you know . . .

Life jackets were invented 200 years ago by a French priest, who lined a vest with cork.

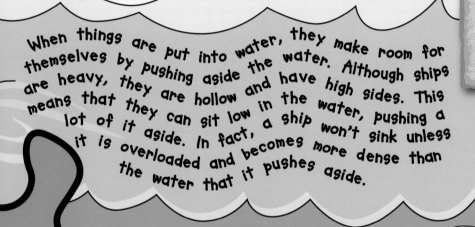

When things are put into water, they make room for themselves by pushing aside the water. Although ships are heavy, they are hollow and have high sides. This means that they can sit low in the water, pushing a lot of it aside. In fact, a ship won't sink unless it is overloaded and becomes more dense than the water that it pushes aside.

If you are nearsighted, distant objects are less clear. If you are farsighted, close objects may seem blurry. People are farsighted or nearsighted because the lenses in their eyes are not exactly the right shape. So they wear glasses or contact lenses to help them see more clearly.

QUICK-QUIZ QUESTIONS

1. What "g" holds you to the ground?

2. Earth is the third planet from the Sun. True or false?

3. What are prominences?

4. How deep underwater can humans dive?

5. What does chlorophyll use to make food for trees?

6. Conifer trees lose their leaves in the winter. True or false?

7. What is metamorphosis?

8. Unscramble RED BIRD WAG to show what castles use to keep enemies out.

9. Where did samurai knights come from?

10. Airplanes are good for the environment. True or false?

11. What helps fight germs in your body?

12. Which is lighter—warm or cold air?

13. Snakes have very good eyesight. True or false?

14. What is the biggest bird on Earth?

15. Unscramble COIN RIFT to show what force helps tires grip.

16. What is a baby kangaroo called?

17. When did the dinosaurs die out?

18. Who invented cement to be used in building roads?

19. Who was king of the gods in ancient Greek stories?

20. Where did the first hot-air balloon ride take place?

21. What is the tallest mountain on Earth?

22. What is pollination?

23. How much of Earth's water is salty?

24. Which sea is the saltiest?

25. Unscramble BE IN EARTH to show what some animals do in the winter.

QUICK-QUIZ
ANSWERS

1. Gravity.

2. True.

3. Flamelike sheets of glowing gas that shoot out from a star.

4. 650 feet (200 meters).

5. Sunlight, water, and carbon dioxide.

6. False. Conifer leaves can withstand the cold winter.

7. When animals change shape and form into something completely different.

8. RED BIRD WAG = drawbridge.

9. Japan.

10. False. They release chemicals that damage Earth's atmosphere.

11. Antibodies produced by the immune system.

12. Warm air.

13. False. Snakes have very bad eyesight.

14. The ostrich.

15. COIN RIFT = friction.

16. A joey.

17. About 65 million years ago.

18. The Romans.

19. Zeus.

20. Paris, France, in 1783.

21. Mount Everest.

22. When grains of pollen are carried from one flower to another so that new seeds can be made.

23. About 97 percent.

24. The Dead Sea.

25. BE IN EARTH = hibernate (sleep through a cold winter).

TRICKY WORDS

ABSORB
To soak up or take in.

ANTARCTICA
Earth's icy, southernmost area around the South Pole.

ANTIBODIES
Tiny parts of the body that are created by the immune system to find and fight germs and keep the body free from illnesses.

ARMOR
A covering that protects a body from harm.

ASTRONAUT
A person who travels into space to find out more about it.

ATMOSPHERE
The layer of gases surrounding a planet. Earth's atmosphere keeps in the heat from the Sun but also keeps out many harmful rays from the Sun.

BACTERIA
Germs that can cause illnesses and infections.

CARBON DIOXIDE
A colorless, invisible gas that animals exhale (breathe out).

CHARIOT
An ancient, horse-drawn vehicle.

EARTH'S CRUST
The outer layer of planet Earth, on which we live.

EMPIRE
A large area of land, usually several countries, ruled by one government. The Romans had a huge empire.

EXTINCT
When not even one of a type of animal or plant is alive.

FORT
A building like a castle that contains armed soldiers.

GAS
Something that isn't solid or liquid. Oxygen is a gas.

GERMS
Tiny living things that can cause illnesses.

GILLS
The breathing parts on an underwater creature. Water is breathed in through gills, which take out the oxygen in the water so that the creature can breathe.

GRAVITY
A force of attraction between objects. This happens in space, for example, where a moon is held in orbit around a planet because the planet has a larger mass.

IMMUNE SYSTEM
The body's system that fights harmful germs by creating antibodies.

JET PROPULSION
When something moves by squirting a rush of water behind it, which pushes it forward.

LUNGS
The organs in the body that help creatures breathe by supplying the body with oxygen.

METEORITE
A rock from space that falls down to Earth.

MULTIPLY
To increase in number.

NERVES
Parts inside the body that sense pain.

ORBIT
The path of an object as it travels around something. Earth orbits the Sun.

OXYGEN
A colorless, invisible gas in air that animals need to breathe in order to live.

PREDATOR
An animal that hunts and eats another animal.

PREY
An animal that is hunted and eaten by another animal.

REFLECT
To bend back light from a surface. A mirror bends back light so that you can see your reflection.

ROMAN
Of an ancient people from Italy who lived around 2,000 years ago in Europe, Africa, and Asia.

SCENT
A smell.

SENSITIVE
Being able to react to one or several of the five senses of touch, taste, smell, sight, or hearing.

SENSOR
A part of an animal's body that detects things for a particular sense, such as taste or smell.

SILK
Fine threads that are made by insects and woven together to make a soft, smooth, and strong material.

SOLAR SYSTEM
The Sun and the objects in space that orbit it, including the eight planets.

STEEL
A strong metal.

TRANSPARENT
Something that is clear or see-through.

VIBRATE
To move back and forth quickly.

WHERE
TO FIND
STUFF

Wow! What an amazing journey! We hope you had as much fun as we did and learned many new things. Who knew that there was so much to discover about "why!" Speaking of "who," we can tell you that we'll soon be going on a few more exciting journeys:

The Book of . . . How?
The Book of . . . What?
The Book of . . . Who?

Look out for these great books! "Who" knows "what" we'll discover . . .

See you soon!